The Servant King

The Servant King

REFLECTIONS IN WORDS AND IMAGES

Paula Clifford

DIMENSIONS
FOR LIVING
NASHVILLE

Original edition published in English under the title *Servant King, The*
by John Hunt Publishing Ltd, New Alresford, Hants, U.K.

Originally published in card form by Christian Aid
Registered charity number 258003

Designed by Andrew Milne Design

Printed by Tien Wah Press Ltd, Singapore

Contents

Above: Detail from *Christ in the Wilderness*
Stanley Spencer

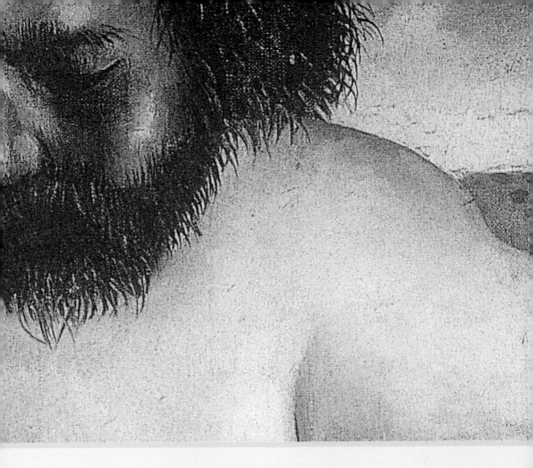

Introduction

*I*n Jesus two separate strands of Old Testament prophecy are fulfilled: the promise of a king to be born 'from the stock of Jesse' (Isaiah 11:1), and Isaiah's foretelling of a mysterious servant, who will be 'despised and rejected,' and subject to untold suffering, in order that he might 'make many righteous' (Isaiah 53:3-11).

The twin image of servant and king is one that dominates our perception of the events of Good Friday and Easter Day. Yet, if we are prepared to see them, these two aspects of Jesus' character and mission are there throughout his earthly ministry, enhancing our

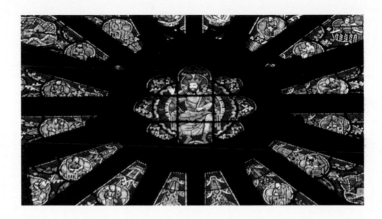

understanding of his words and actions during those three years.

The idea of a king who also serves, and who suffers in serving, has been a source of strength to Christians in countries where oppression and hardship are basic facts of life. The Asian Christian Women's Conference in 1990 declared: 'Through [Christ's] suffering messiahship, he creates a new humanity.' It seems particularly appropriate then, that this Lent book should focus on this theme, and illustrate it through art from around the world.

In recent years the developing countries of South America have been the source of Liberation Theology, which has offered the church a fresh approach to the Bible. By adopting the perspective of the disadvantaged, Liberation Theologians have highlighted the radical nature of the Christian gospel and the hope that it offers to the world's poor. Some of their insights are included in the notes to the biblical texts in this book.

I have chosen to combine words and pictures as a starting point for personal reflection on the Servant King during Lent. But this is only a beginning. If you will allow him, God will direct your thoughts to a fresh understanding of the gospel message and inspire you to pray and act for his world.

The images are mainly, but not exclusively, by artists from the developing world and the different styles of all the artists echo the variety of cultures in which they have been formed. They are not intended to be representative of Christian art across the world. Instead, the images have been chosen for their less familiar perspective and the new light they throw on events in the Gospel narratives.

The choice of the English artist Stanley Spencer for Ash Wednesday deserves comment. In 1939 Spencer turned from secular subject matter to biblical themes, and conceived the idea of creating 40 painted panels, one for each day of Lent. In the end he completed only nine, each on the subject of 'Christ in the Wilderness.' Christ is portrayed as interacting between the two aspects of God's creation - human beings and the natural world. Spencer's simple, direct style blends in remarkably well with the images that follow and sets the tone for them. Like them, it is powerful and thought provoking and a fruitful basis for meditating on God's world.

The images are intended to stimulate your thoughts and prayers. The comments facing each image

are a way in to reflection. Allow the artists' work to direct your imagination. You might find it helpful to focus on a particular detail and some of the details may be unexpected. For instance, in the cleansing of the Temple (Lent 3), the well-dressed men are being driven out by young people in jeans, not the other way round. Do you find this surprising?

The figures depicted are from various ethnic backgrounds. How do you react to them? Do they help you understand what it is to be a servant – or a king?

Following each image and meditation you will find short notes on readings appointed in the Revised Common Lectionary, Year B and a prayer. The notes are related to each other through the theme of the Servant King and are linked to their corresponding images by the reading itself. The notes may therefore be used in conjunction with the images, or independently. The notes are probably best used on the specific days themselves as an aid to understanding the Bible passage.

The short prayer can be used on its own, or you could add in a prayer of your own stemming from your reflection on the image. So, for Lent 3, you might move on to pray for young people, both at home and overseas, for their ideals and their future.

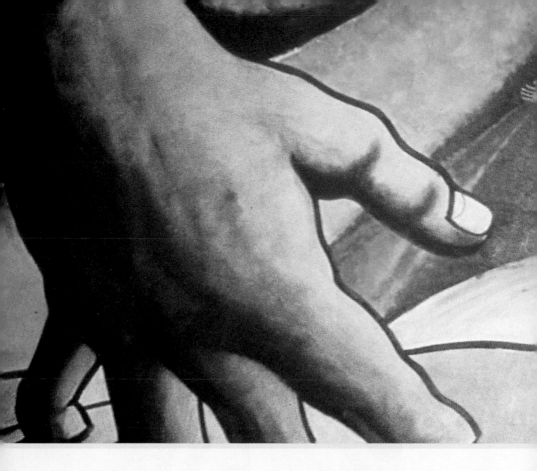

Above: Detail from *Mural, Church of St. Rose of Lima, Peru*
Edwin Quintana

Meditations

ASH WEDNESDAY

'Is not this the fast that I choose...'

Jesus is alone with his thoughts, alone in a barren desert. In Spencer's picture he holds one of the less attractive of God's creatures: a scorpion. The creature can move freely, with no risk of being trodden underfoot.

This is Jesus the servant. He is already God's servant, with the mission to bring good news of his kingdom. Now, at the start of his long period of fasting, he prepares to become the servant of humankind, caring for all people, accepting their burdens, bearing their punishment. And in the meantime he contemplates the wonderful work of God's hands, in a lowly life form, and serves it by offering his protection.

STANLEY SPENCER

Christ in the Wilderness: The Scorpion (1939)

Ash Wednesday: Isaiah 58:1-12

GIVING UP SOMETHING has become deep-rooted in our understanding of Lent. But we may have our own reasons for giving up certain things, which raises the question: Who stands to benefit, us or God and our neighbor?

God's words through Isaiah are a rebuke to Israel for the way people behave towards others, while faithfully carrying out their religious duties. At that time, fasting was part of a ritual commemorating the disastrous events that overtook Jerusalem before the exile into Babylon. And Isaiah takes people to task for observing the rite without fully understanding the point of it, and allowing fasting to become a habit, which bore little relation to anything else in their lives (see also Zechariah 7:3).

One positive effect of fasting is that it can help us focus our minds more closely on God. But there are other things which

God wants people to give up besides food: to give up quarrelling, behaving unjustly, and putting oneself before everyone else; and instead to care for the hungry, the homeless, the naked and the oppressed.

So 'giving up' is transformed into another kind of action – 'giving out': serving other people, after the example of Jesus himself. Giving food to the hungry and clothes to the naked are actions that Jesus will see as characteristic of those who are judged worthy to come into his kingdom, because 'just as you did it to one of the least of these who are members of my family, you did it to me' (Matthew 25:40).

PRAYER

Lord Jesus, may I learn to be a better servant
this Lent.
May I follow your example in serving God and all
whom he loves, all to whom he has given life.

LENT ONE

'The kingdom of God has come near'

In the wilderness, Jesus and Satan stare at each other, in almost unbearable intimacy, while we see the devil's knowing smile. Jesus cradles in his hand the stone that he alone has the power to turn into bread. The birds wait impatiently.

The devil tries to persuade Jesus to take a short cut: to impose his kingdom in a way people can easily understand, forcing them to believe in his power. That way he could remain aloof from ordinary human beings and avoid the pain that lies ahead.

Through facing his own agonizing choices, Jesus fully understands ours.

AN DONG-SOOK

Temptation of Christ

Lent One: Mark 1:9-15

BY OPENING WITH WORDS from Old Testament prophets (Mark 1:2-3), Mark has told us at once that the Messiah is coming. Yet when Jesus appears he seems hardly to match up to expectations. Jesus was from a provincial area where people spoke differently and were suspected of peculiar religious and political activities. Nothing good could come out of Galilee (see Nathanael's question in John 1:46). Then Jesus receives John's 'baptism of repentance,' not because he was sinful but so that he might stand alongside those who are. His baptism is a deliberate act of submission before his ministry begins – a ministry that will end with another such act: the crucifixion.

In response to this, God's voice confirms that Jesus is indeed the long-awaited King: 'Thou art my beloved Son.' The words are from Psalm 2:7 and had traditionally been used when Israel's kings were anointed, indicating that the new king was to be treated by God as his own child. Yet, as the only Son of God, Jesus was to be a king with a difference, and the detail of John's arrest is an indication of the way of suffering in store for Him.

Jesus' first public words reveal that God's kingdom is now no longer a distant promise. But the good news that the kingdom is already a reality is announced in a wholly unexpected context.

'Jesus, a Galilean, proclaims his message in a place that was unimportant and marginal. It is from among the poor and despised that the message comes of the universal love that the God of Jesus Christ has for humankind,' as the Peruvian theologian Gustavo Gutierrez puts it.

PRAYER

Lord Jesus, help me to lay down the things that tempt me; to tear my eyes away from people who take me along the wrong path; and not to give in to the pressures around me. Be with me in my wilderness.

LENT TWO

'Let them deny themselves and take up their cross and follow me'

Here Christ is given the form of a Nicaraguan worker in his everyday working clothes. His effort, as he toils up the hill bearing the full weight of the cross, reflects his everyday labor. His expression is one of grim determination.

The colors of the sky foreshadow the darkness to come. The purple tones are suggestive of the royal cloak which the mocking soldiers put on Jesus. The bare landscape offers no relief from the upward struggle or from the bleakness of the whole scene.

To take up the cross of Jesus is to carry it ourselves in our own particular circumstances. So Christ himself becomes part of our everyday lives.

Mural, Church of Santa Maria de los Angeles, Managua
(ARTIST UNKNOWN)
Photo: Christian Aid/Richard Baggott

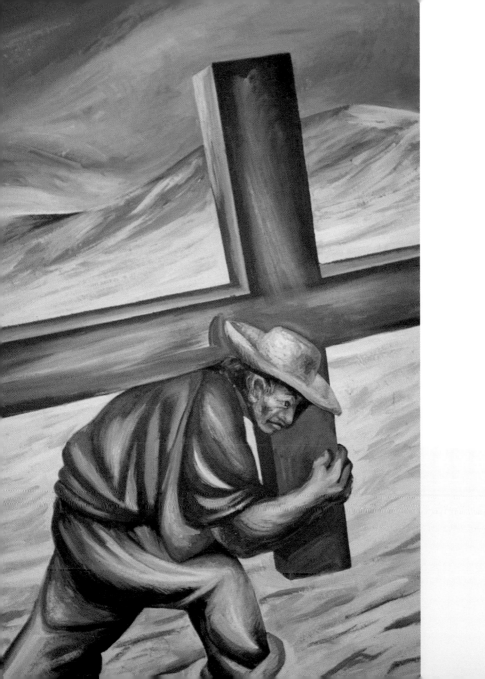

APPOINTED READINGS FOR LENT

Lent Two: Mark 8:31-39

THE TEMPTATION to take power the easy way was never far away. At Caesarea Philippi it was Peter, one of Jesus' closest friends, who tried to argue him out of the way of suffering. Jesus' words are harsh, 'Get behind me, Satan!' Peter needed to see how wrong he was, but maybe he had touched a raw nerve as well.

For Peter the rebuke must have been doubly hurtful, coming so soon after his great moment of insight into who Jesus was: 'You are the Christ.' The problem was that it was only a partial insight. Peter had recognized Jesus as Christ, the 'anointed one,' but he had assumed Jesus would be a king like any other. That is something he could not be allowed to think, even for a moment.

So Peter and the others have to be taught that Jesus' kingship and his kingdom are very different from those of the world. The demands of the kingdom are crazy by the world's standards. To 'deny yourself' is not simply to give things up. It means not having yourself at the center of your life any longer; it may mean risking life itself, and even being like the condemned criminal who had to carry the cross-beam of a cross to the place of execution. Recognizing Jesus as King can be a dangerous thing. So Jean-Marc Ela, a theologian from Cameroon, writes of discovering God in Christ in a world where 'God speaks to us and summons us by the facts of injustice and by every situation of misery.' In other words, it will not always be a comfortable experience.

PRAYER

You are the God of the poor,

The down-to-earth human God,

God who sweats in the street,

God with a sunburnt face.

NICARAGUAN MASS (OPENING SONG)

LENT THREE

'Zeal for thy house will consume me'

It was a passionate Jesus who took a cattle whip and drove traders out of the Temple. His actions are represented in a scene set in a Nicaraguan church in the 1980s. Young people fighting for democracy are depicted here showing similar passion and using the same whips, as they drive out the formally dressed men who represent the old order of power and privilege.

On the walls of the building, images of the crucifixion bear witness to the cost of Jesus' actions. And as in their passion for a new order the young people take the same risks as their Lord, so too does the church, which has chosen to place itself firmly on the side of the poor.

MARITA GUEVARA

Jesus drives the merchants from the Temple

Lent Three: John 2:13-22

WE CAN IMAGINE the disciples' reactions to the dramatic events in the Temple. They might have been excited, angry or embarrassed and bewildered. What did it all mean? That at least would only become completely clear after Jesus' death and resurrection.

But for now, Jesus' actions are devastating. He attacks both the long-established forms of Temple worship and, indirectly, the worshipers themselves. Because, in his kingdom, worship is to be very different. The kingdom is to be marked by spiritual worship.

As Jesus tells the woman of Samaria, 'God is spirit, and those who worship him must worship in spirit and in truth' (John 4:24).

So the sacrificial system, a fundamental part of Temple worship, has to be done away with. And for a while Jesus makes normal worship impossible, with the animals and the money to buy them all in disarray.

As for the worshipers, Jesus' kingdom is for everyone. So Jesus lashes out against signs of non-Jews being excluded. In particular he targets the moneychangers, since Gentile currency was not acceptable in the Temple.

He also challenges the timeless problem of the abuse of power. Here, religious power is being used as a means of profiteering and thus of exploiting the poor.

In setting this incident near the start of Jesus' ministry, John gives us a key to understanding some of what lies ahead. Jesus' understanding of himself as the true dwelling-place of God – a dwelling which when destroyed would rise again – was bound to lead to regular clashes with Jewish religious leaders, and, ultimately, to terrible suffering.

PRAYER

Thank you, Lord Jesus, for your passionate commitment to truth and justice. May I not be afraid to stand up for what is right and support those who follow your example.

'God so loved the world...'

There is no limit to God's love for us, a love which is reflected, however weakly, in the feelings of human parents for their children. It starts at the moment of creation. This Peruvian artist depicts human life emerging from the desert: with his left hand God scoops man and woman out of the sand, which is molded like a giant seed.

God commits himself to the unending work of shelter and protection. His right hand behind the couple protects them from the sun and chaotic forces of nature. Their light comes straight from God himself.

That was the beginning. God's ultimate act of love was to give us his Son, so that any created being who believes in him might have God's final gift: everlasting life.

EDWIN QUINTANA

Mural, Church of St. Rose of Lima, Ica, Peru

Photo: Paul Place

Lent Four: John 3:14-21

FOR ISRAEL in the wilderness, the serpent was a sign of life. If people had the faith and obedience to look up at the serpent that Moses had set up on a pole (Numbers 21:9), they would remain alive and safe. But that salvation was only for this life and was restricted to an insignificant group of people isolated from the rest of the world. The cross on which Jesus was to be lifted up would be much more than that. It would be for the whole world, not just a small part of it, and it would be salvation for eternal life. Unlike the serpent, the cross is not just a sign of salvation: it is salvation.

The cross is also the sign of Jesus' glory. Through his crucifixion, that terrible form of torture becomes identified not with darkness but with light. From now on it is at the cross that people will find 'the true light which lightens everyone' (John 1:9) -

Jesus the Word. In all this, God has taken the first step: our salvation is his plan. This in turn places a responsibility on us to identify ourselves with his purpose. 'We find God,' says Gutierrez, 'to the extent that we make our own God's plan for history and our lives.'

The cross represents the greatest act of self-sacrifice the world has known. But that doesn't mean sacrifice is absent from the lives of ordinary people. It is part and parcel of the love of parents for their children, and however fallible we know ourselves to be, the lack of selfishness in our parents' love for us, and ours for our children may well surprise us.

PRAYER

Heavenly Father, thank you for your loving creation
and protection of all living things. Open my heart
to love as you love, that I may reflect your true
light in the world.

'If a grain of wheat dies, it bears much fruit'

A seed dreams of becoming a tree – a dream of its future glory. As a seed in a pot it is vulnerable, its tiny stem is all too fragile. But once in the ground it will become secure and strong, a place where little doves can come and rest. Even when it sheds its leaves with the season it remains a safe place of refuge.

Jesus' future glory depends on his being willing to be vulnerable. Like the seed once it has fallen to the ground, Jesus after his death will be raised to new life and will become the strength and refuge of all who, like the doves, seek him out.

The source of that strength – as the bare shape of the tree reminds us – is the cross.

Rêve d'une Germe

PASCAL MERISIER (HAITI)

A Seed's Dream

Lent Five: John 12:20-33

IF A SEED IS TO GROW, it can't stay in the form of a seed. Jesus takes this basic truth and applies it to the whole of Christian discipleship. His followers in this world can't remain apart if they are to bear fruit both in their own spiritual growth and in bringing others to him.

If people are to follow Christ, the Servant King, they can't stay as they are. To prove that these aren't just empty words, Jesus applies them to himself.

He asks nothing of his followers that he's not first prepared to do himself. So if Jesus is to be 'glorified' he can't stay as he is: he has to suffer and die. And so he will.

It's not just individuals who are called to change. God's people as a whole are being called by Jesus to transform themselves. He has already taken action against the Temple moneychangers who were there because Gentile coins were unacceptable. The arrival of the Greeks is suggestive of a still greater change. As the day of Jesus' death approaches, so too does the time when all people will know him. The cross, the sign of Christ's glory, will become central for people of all nations.

Today we are not finished with change. Not only individuals, but the church itself may need to change, to be reminded that Jesus is Lord for all times and all places, and to reflect on how we proclaim this. The Sri Lankan theologian Tissa Balasuriya talks about the need for a Christian 'cultural revolution' within the church and its theology. There has to be nothing less than 'a fundamental reorientation of the thinking of Christians to meet the challenges of our time.'

PRAYER

Thank you, Lord Jesus, for becoming weak and vulnerable for my sake, for giving me total security through the cross.

'Hosanna!'

The crowds who met Jesus were overwhelming. They weren't clustered in orderly groups, waving polite little flags. They were a barely controlled mob making a deafening noise.

They had taken whole branches with them to greet the king. A Japanese flower arranger imagines the concrete of the city disappearing beneath their palms. Despite the beauty, there's a veiled threat: are they palms or are they spears? The city will not allow popular enthusiasm to dominate it for long, and its ancient traditions and prejudices will soon make themselves felt again.

The cross is already a barely concealed presence, and all too soon the hidden violence will be unleashed as the crowd turns against Jesus: 'Crucify him!'

GATE OTA

Palm Sunday

Passion/Palm Sunday: John 12:12-16

AT JERUSALEM THERE WAS CHAOS and confusion. Jesus had his own crowd of followers with him - people who had witnessed his last and greatest miracle, the raising of Lazarus. They clashed head on with the hordes of pilgrims who were swarming out of the city.

These people thought they knew what was going on. They thought they were at last going to meet their Messiah, the king who would set them free from Roman rule and lead them into a new golden age. The words they shouted were from Psalm 118, a psalm traditionally sung at the festival, which gave expression to their hopes for the nation's future. But there was a jarring note: their king was coming on a donkey, a sign not of royal military power but of peace.

The disciples were confused too. Jesus' teaching about his kingdom probably hadn't led them to expect this. They didn't see how the scriptural understanding of kingship fitted with Jesus and with the expectations of the crowd. They couldn't yet see that Jesus, their true king, was fulfilling both the prophecy of

Zechariah (Zechariah 9:9) and the servant prophecy of Isaiah. The king had to suffer and die so that his people could witness his unique glory. Only later would the disciples understand, when they received the gift of his Holy Spirit.

The confusion at Jerusalem had to do with conflicting ideas about the kingship of Jesus and the nature of his kingdom. Jon Sobrino, a Spanish-born theologian working in San Salvador, defines the reign of God as 'that situation in which human beings have genuine knowledge of God and establish right and justice toward the poor.' This is certainly a far cry from some of the ideas floating around on that first Palm Sunday.

PRAYER

Lord Jesus, forgive us when our enthusiasm and
warmth for you turns to neglect or wounding
hostility.
As the crowds cried out 'Hosanna,' so we pray
'Save us!'

'Lord, are you going to wash my feet?'

The disciple might have made it easier for Jesus by holding his legs out in front of him. Instead, Jesus has to reach down so that he is bent almost double, his head bowed, in the most abject position of a slave.

Here Jesus truly sets majesty aside, as the color of his robes causes him to blend not with the sky above but with the ground.

The disciple takes the place of the master, his head at the top of the triangle, in which the whole drama is enclosed, emphasizing his apparent superiority.

The Indian artist has chosen this shape to represent the leaf of the bodhi tree, sacred to Buddhists, thereby adding a further cultural dimension to Jesus' unforgettable action.

JYOTI SAHI
Washing the Feet

Maundy Thursday: John 13:1-17, 31b-35

WHEN JESUS WASHES his disciples' feet he is quite unmistakably taking on the role of a servant. It's with this act of service that the process of his 'glorification' begins. From now on the paradox of the king who is servant, or the servant who is king, becomes increasingly evident. However humble the task (washing feet), however great the humiliation (mocking, scourging and public execution), Jesus the King remains in sovereign control.

His full knowledge of the significance of his action now and of what is shortly to take place contrasts with the disciples' confusion and ignorance. Jesus' words carry full authority: 'You call me Teacher and Lord – and you are right, for that is what I am.'

Jesus the King demonstrates his authority further in giving his disciples a commandment. What's new about it is that Christian love is to be love as Jesus himself has modeled it, in reversing natural roles and becoming everyone's servant.

This commandment gives new meaning to love. It will be love of the kind that St Paul describes: being patient, kind, not insisting on its own way (1 Corinthians 13). It's a love that doesn't

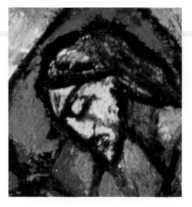

come ready made and it is not always easy to show. As Bakole wa Ilunga, Archbishop of Kananga, Zaire, puts it, such love 'is not a feeling of natural sympathy or natural solidarity. It is an attitude we must learn and a task we must carry out at cost to ourselves.' The ultimate cost of such love is revealed at Calvary.

PRAYER

Lord Jesus, may I learn to follow your example and wash the feet of others; and may I gratefully accept their service when they seek to wash mine.

'My servant... shall be exalted and lifted up'

The night before he died, Jesus prayed to his Father, 'Glorify your Son so that the Son may glorify you.'

Christ finds glory on the cross. The artist uses red and white as symbols of life and death. The colors flow together in his body and in the robes of his followers. Black represents their shared suffering.

Beside the cross are African martyrs who have given their lives to serve their crucified king. As yet their heads are bowed, their eyes downcast, their hands hang at their sides. By contrast, the raised arms and nailed hands of Jesus are spread out in love and blessing to his world. He holds his head high, his eyes are wide open as he offers an eternal welcome to his lost and suffering children.

ENGELBERT MVENG (DOUALA, CAMEROON)

Christ in Majesty

APPOINTED READINGS FOR LENT

Good Friday: Isaiah 52:13 – 53:12

WHO HAS BELIEVED what we have heard?' People were astonished at the wretchedness of God's servant: how could God have chosen such a despicable figure for special exaltation? At a different time, other people would be equally amazed that God's Son should undergo the humiliating and painful process of death by crucifixion – the most terrible form of capital punishment ever devised.

We don't know the original identity of Isaiah's servant: he may have represented the whole nation. But whoever he was, the prophet depicts his life as dominated by extremes of suffering. He was an outsider, rejected because he was disfigured, and the object of all kinds of persecution. When he died they buried him with the wicked, misjudged and misunderstood. Later, people realized what they had done. They came to see that the servant had taken their punishment on himself. And he had done so willingly. 'He poured out his soul to death,' he did nothing by halves.

The early church soon came to see the servant figure as fore-shadowing the suffering and death of Jesus. And St Paul understood that Jesus the King had to go to an even greater extreme than the servant in Isaiah: 'Though he was in the form of God, he emptied himself, taking the form of a servant... ' (Philippians 2:6-7). In order to bear our sorrows - the pain of yesterday, today and tomorrow - Jesus did nothing less than set aside his divinity and became one of us.

'Jesus is the representative of all the human beings throughout the world and down the centuries who have suffered violence, pain, and death from their own brethren. It is their cause that he pleads with his God' (Archbishop Bakole wa Ilunga of Zaire).

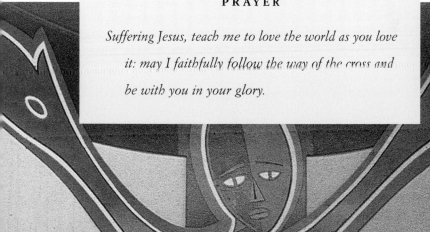

PRAYER

Suffering Jesus, teach me to love the world as you love it: may I faithfully follow the way of the cross and be with you in your glory.

EASTER SUNDAY

'He has been raised'

After the darkness and brutality of death by crucifixion comes the awesome light of resurrection. The women who came to the tomb early on the first Easter morning were exhausted, worn out by grief, lack of sleep and fear. To find the tomb empty only increased their anxiety.

In Matthew's Gospel the terrifying presence of the angel in the tomb is followed by the heart-stopping appearance of Jesus himself.

An artist from Zimbabwe imagines the two Marys bathed in a light which falls on their drawn and frightened faces and on the now useless spice jars. Yet even in their sorry state Jesus sends them out, trusting them to proclaim the Easter message: that Jesus, the light of the world, has overcome darkness for ever.

GEORGE NENE

The risen Christ reveals himself first to the two women

APPOINTED READINGS

Easter Sunday: Mark 16:1-8

CHRIST IS RISEN from the dead. Mark's Gospel stresses the emotion that this unique event aroused in the first people to hear about it. The news was heart stopping and terrifying to the three women, who realized they were witnessing the power of God in a way never before experienced in human history. For the time being, at least, they were speechless.

There's another extraordinary thing about the resurrection, not only in Mark's version but in all the Gospels: it was women who knew about it first, women who saw the risen Lord before anyone else. And this, despite the fact that in Jewish tradition, as in the majority of cultures, women are, or have been, regarded predominantly as those whose role is to serve. Indeed, throughout his life on earth, Jesus, the genuine servant of all, showed care and respect for women, giving them back their dignity, just as he did for other people who were seen as being of little worth: foreigners and slaves, the poor and the sick.

Across the world women today continue to draw great comfort from Jesus' treatment of women. As Yong Ting Jin, a Malaysian theologian, writes: 'Women were the first in faith, in terms of both their coming to faith and their quality of faith. They played a decisive role in the directing of God's Liberation history.' It is also an inspiration for the future. She comments: 'Women must today rediscover their original and distinctive role in the Gospel.'

On Easter Day the servant at last reclaims his full majesty. And his resurrection offers to women and men, poor and rich, a source of unending hope.

PRAYER

Risen Lord Jesus, may your light shine out on your world this Easter. May we set weariness aside and rush to pass on the good news of your resurrection life.

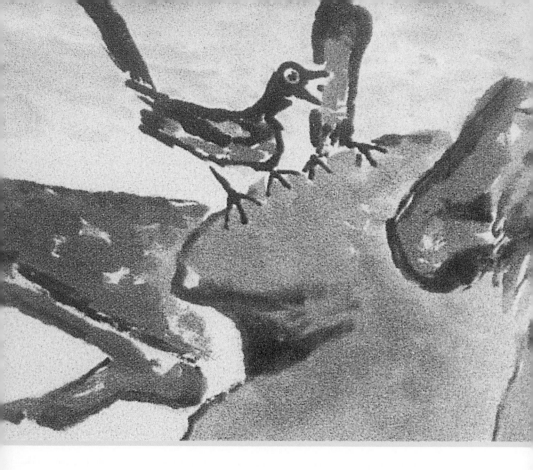

Above: Detail from *Temptation of Christ*
An Dong-Sook

Reference

Acknowledgments

Ash Wednesday: *Stanley Spencer, Christ in the Wilderness*: The Scorpion (1939). Oil on canvas (56 x 56 cm). Collection Art Gallery of Western Australia. Reproduced by permission.

Lent One: *An Dong-Sook* (Korea), *Temptation of Christ* (watercolor 1990), in Masao Takenaka and Ron O'Grady, The Bible Through Asian Eyes, Pace Publishing (Auckland, New Zealand) in association with the Asian Christian Art Association (Kyoto, Japan), 1991. Reproduced by permission.

Lent Two; Cover: *Mural from the Church of Santa Maria de los Angeles*, Managua, Nicaragua. Photo: Christian Aid/Richard Baggott.

Lent Three: *Jesus drives the merchants from the Temple*, by *Mari'ta Guevara*, in The Gospel in Art by the Peasants of Solentiname (eds Philip & Sally Scharper), Orbis Books (New York), 1984. One of a number of paintings dating from 1981-82, when people returned to a remote village in Nicaragua after Somoza's destruction. Reproduced by permission.

Lent Four: *Mural by Edwin Quintana from the Parish Church of Saint Rose of Lima* in the shanty town of The Lord of Kurin in the city of Ica, Peru. Photo: Paul Place

Lent Five: *Pascal Merisier* (Port-au-Prince, Haiti), *A Seed's Dream*. Original painting (76 x 60cm).

Passion/Palm Sunday: *Gato Ota* (Japan), *Palm Sunday*, in The Bible Through Asian Eyes.

Maundy Thursday: *Jyoti Sahi* (Bangalore, India), *Washing the Feet*, in The Bible Through Asian Eyes.

Good Friday: *Engelbert Mveng* (Cameroon), *Christ in Majesty*, fresco on the apse of the Chapel Libermann College, Douala, in Hans-Ruedi Weber, On a Friday Noon: Meditations under the Cross, World Council of Churches (Geneva), 1979. Permission applied for.

Easter Sunday: *George Nene* (Zimbabwe), *The risen Christ reveals himself first to the two women*, in Welcome to Zimbabwe, World Council of Churches (Geneva), 1998. Permission applied for.

References

Balasuriya, Tissa in *Liberation Theology: An Introductory Reader*
(eds C. Cadorette, M. Giblin, M. J. Legge and M. H. Snyder) (Orbis Books)
1992, p. 41 (Lent 5)

Ela, Jean-Marc, 'The Granary is Empty' in *My Faith as an African* (1988)
reprinted in Liberation Theology: An Introductory Reader, p. 73 (Lent 2)

Gutierrez, Gustavo, *The God of Life* (Orbis Books) 1991, pp. 67 and 99
(Lent Four and Lent One)

Ilunga, Bakole wa, *Paths of Liberation: A Third World Spirituality* (1978)
(trans. M. O'Connell, Orbis Books, 1984), p.104 (Maundy Thursday and
Good Friday)

Sobrino, Jon in *Liberation Theology: An Introductory Reader*, p.111
(Palm Sunday)

Yong Ting Jin in *Liberation Theology: An Introductory Reader*, p. 201
(Easter Day)